Balancing Act

For Marie,
as we honor our mothers

Bob Longoni
May 6, 2016

Balancing Act

poems

Robert Longoni

Bernardo Cristiani Taiz

Moon Pony Press

2015

Published by:
Moon Pony Press
c/o Meg Files
PO Box 85394
Tucson AZ 85754

ISBN 978-1-931638-08-1

Library of Congress Control Number: 2015945908

Cover art from a water color by Lee Taiz

Authors' Photographs:
  Bernardo Cristiani Taiz © Danielle Ramirez
  Robert Longoni © Angela Longoni

Book Design by Leila Joiner

Edited by Nancy Wall and Meg Files

Printed in the U.S.A. on sustainably harvested paper.

Text set in Minion.

In Memory of

Steve Orlen
1942 - 2010
tough, honest, kind,
his work always one of discovery

Lois Shelton
1932 - 2015
whose gracious generosity of spirit
enabled all in the world of poetry

Acknowledgments

for Robert Longoni *RL*

In *The Blue Guitar,* Fall 2014:
  "Alaska"
  "A Place in the Sun"
  "Distance"
  "Morning Stretch"
  "Mourning Doves"
  "Windows"

In *Woodpiles,* Moon Pony Press, 1997:
  "Lacking Anything Swift"

To be published in *Zocalo,* Tucson, Arizona, November 2015:
  "Learning How It's Done at the Bocce Club"

for Bernardo Cristiani Taiz *BCT*

In *Lasting: Poems on Aging,* Pima Press, 2005:
  "Balancing Act"

In *Digging with My Hands,* Pima Press, 2006:
  "Confluence"
  "Crossing the Line"
  "Fortune Cookie"
  "Old love,"
  "The Scream"
  "Tsunami"

Many thanks to:
  Our editors, Nancy Wall and Meg Files, for their guidance,
    patience, and hard work, precious time from their busy
    lives
  Barrie Ryan and Susan North, for their abiding
    encouragement and support of our work, in short for
    their love
  Sue Myers, without whose help this book would still be
    chicken scratch across reams of yellow notepaper
  Tony Apicella, for his enduring friendship

Contents

III   Afloat Between Margins: The Soul's Circus

About the Authors

for Vivian, the children,
all who bring the light

RL

for family, friends
who keep the coals alive

BCT

I

The Lemonade Tree

Two Old Men on a Bench

I promise Bernardo that if he dies first
I'll write him a poem. He says the same
for me, joking it will never happen that way.
I'm not so sure, I counter; your mother lived
longer than mine. And anyone who endures
all that has tried to take you down can
outlast those of us who merely survive.

Before he wrapped up his second collection
he thought he was hanging on for that.
He even got down to a few cigarettes a day.
Now that he's quit totally, I remind him
that should be enough to get him another book.
And what can I count on, who never smoked?

Later he'll think of something else to say,
and I'll be ready with another question.
We'll laugh again, finding new ways
to keep going. Two foolish old men,
one rearranging scraps of his life,
the other dancing while dodging beams.

Balancing Act

I didn't know then
that all we got was a life,
that there were no guarantees.

And why should I
when I could balance a broom
on my chin or walk it

from my little finger to my thumb,
a child's nimble steps beneath that axis
defying the force of gravity?

I was reminded of this in the shower
today, when I tilted my head back
to rinse shampoo from my hair.

Eyes closed, teetering under the weight
of decades, that dizzying acceleration of age,
I realized how little time is left

in front of me and what frightening shapes
might lurk beyond the next turn.
The years shift things, as they must,

gravity leering like a gargoyle.
Thankfully, suspense dims, though
whatever order there may have been

is constantly open to revision.
Like an old tree,
its roots exposed by the elements,

we become top-heavy,
and why shouldn't we
when so much has gone straight to the heart?

RL

Memories

When you reach a certain age
you begin to think of them
collectively as your life

as if they were all threads
of the same fabric or tiles in a
mosaic. Or episodes in a dull novel.

But when you try to line them up
to get a glimpse of the whole story,
you find out they're more like

hermit crabs scattered on a beach,
each encapsuled in its own moment,
or they're words in a dictionary

and the best you can do
is something like filing them
alphabetically: Under A

the move to Arizona, alone on a train
through the flooded midwest at sixteen.
Under F the First, the earliest recalled,

when naked you jumped from a washtub
down open stairs to the sidewalk and raced
a step ahead of your mother

to an open field. The Field
where futility began and ended.
Music lessons, abandoned,

awkwardly following Marriage.
Under Q, alone, a Quadruple bypass.
Maybe that way, you tell yourself, you'll know →

how close you're getting to Z
as you watch the last of them crawl,
gripping and sliding in unison.

Lollipops and Superman

I learned to hate cursive
in Miss Cromie's second grade class,
copying ad infinitum the letters—
yes, upper and lower case—
that marched across the wall
on posters just above the blackboard.

I held that fat pencil
with all my might
until a bump rose
on the middle finger
of my right hand,
a crater remaining there still.

Dotted lines paralleled
the axis of the alphabet
and I bore down,
my jaw clenched,
to get the eye of the *L*
just high enough, the belly of the *G*
just low enough,
touching what looks to me now
like a barbed-wire fence,
beyond which lay a meadow and brook
where every creature from the ark
might get its fill.

I learned also to dislike drawing,
that battleax scolding me regularly
because my trees looked like lollipops—
lemon, lime, cherry, orange—
unattached, soaring above the ground
with the birds and clouds and kites,
with smoke which circled from a chimney below. →

I knew, of course,
about this good earth's bounty,
my brother and I—
with the first basic penknife
our grandfather taught us to use—
shaving a thin slice
from the knuckle of a sassafras root
which inched across the sandy soil
before diving toward water
and beyond that maybe China.

But what could I say
to someone so much older
so much more experienced,
other than a rehash
of that scary story about the fall,
when we were banished from the garden,
sin descending upon the world like fog,
death and mummies skulking close behind?

I guess I could have told her
that I simply wanted to fly
like Superman beyond the sharp boundaries
with the bees and butterflies,
scribbling across a perfectly blue sky
just above the lilac and lavender,
the wild rose, the honeysuckle.

RL

Learning How It's Done at the Bocce Club

Saturday mornings at the Sons of Italy
we watched them in action—
grandfathers, uncles, and their
Canadian friends from the textile mills.

Legs wobbling, pipes or cigarettes dangling
from their lips, they never spilled their beer,
swore a lot—in skillful Italian,
clumsy English, intimate French—
glancing at us without looking our way,
pretending they didn't mean the words.

But we knew everything they did
meant something, though we
didn't know what, so we went on
gaping at them as if they were movie stars

and mimicked them all week after school
in the gravel lot behind the cotton mill—
wobbling up to an imaginary line, swearing in three
languages—safe from frowning spinster teachers,

giggling huddled girls: sure of ourselves
as we would never be again.

Shame

It was the last straw:
she had to get his attention.

So the second grader stood at the corner,
not much taller than a fire hydrant,
cowering behind a placard which read,
"I was rude to my teacher.
I'll make good choices from now on."

His mom had wanted to turn up the heat
crumple him like newsprint
to smolder under the magnifying glass of shame.

But in that bunker we call the heart,
he knew he would not be
the first child to fear
that his parents' imperfections
might be his own.

Perhaps he too would forget the snarl
from the grill of every passing car,
the snicker of the sidewalk beneath his feet,
the tears pocking his cheeks like a plague.

RL

Dante and Me

At twelve I knew some Italian girls.
Tina, my age, an innocent flirt,
and Teresa, older, who wore
white blouses with rounded collars.
But no one named Beatrice.

My parents, though they understood
the dialect, would have confused *la vita nuova*
with the life they found in America.
Besides, they never had a girl
they could use the name for.

So I asked around and learned
there was an actress by that name,
a famous author of children's books,
and a couple of society women in Providence.
But even with all that desire,

I was deficient in piety, or imagination,
finding it hard to think of them
as genuine poets obviously could:
closer to my age, naked and holy
at the same time under a skimpy red robe.

Splatter

She is beautiful
in her charcoal-gray slacks
and black turtleneck,
auburn hair
sweeping to her waist.

And then,
on the pavement
there in front of Walgreen's
she spits...
with the deftness of a shortstop,
the ritual
of a compulsive kid
avoiding the cracks
on his way to school.

The air around me
stiffens like shellac
and I duck
down into holiday thoughts
as if to avoid
the splatter of judgment,
as if to escape
the cries of this world.

For the Sister I Never Had

While I'm still alive, I should tell you
I've often wondered what it would have been like
to have you in the family. Especially since
Mom wanted it so, dressing our little brother
like a girl until he was five.

Now that my life is filled out with a wife,
two daughters, and three daughters-in-law,
I see something of you every day, yet I miss you
more than ever, big sister of my dreams,
second mother who didn't panic

when I split my head against a tree,
sympathetic buffer between Dad
and me. I would have let you read
a bedtime story, sneak me a candy bar,
ride my bike, even feed my rabbit

when I was away. And now you'd be
retired from medicine or politics,
a self-sufficient widow in Cleveland,
and that would give me reason
to go there, a place I've never been.

The Lemonade Tree

The little boy was serious
when he spotted the tree
heavy with lemons,
some as big as grapefruit.

"Mister, is that your lemonade tree?"
he asked from the curb,
eyeing it up and down, around,
as he might his first Ferris wheel.

There's a children's story,
I thought, and said as much,
the boy still straddling his bicycle,
entranced by the magic, a sleight
I couldn't remember how to do.

"Will I be in it?" he asked,
leaning forward over the handlebars
like someone who measures distance
with anything but years.

"You bet, it's your story,"
I trailed off, imagining something epic
as I picked a few beauties
from high in the branches beyond his reach—

those closest the sun,
those beyond betrayal,
those that would offer no hint
of the thorns to come,
their juice simply sparkling like sequins
on that theatre of a face.

I showed him how to carry the bounty
in the apron of his T-shirt
and realized that all I could pull
from a top hat now was words
as I tried to pedal backwards
into my own old story—
one so awesome it had seemed then
to spill from a frosted pitcher
whose handle I held,
ice cubes clinking,
spinning like soda-fountain stools,
as dizzying and benevolent as the stars.

RL

Pigeons

When my father brought two home
to start a flock in the garage,
I ran my fingers through softness,
then stood before their cage
watching the light in their eyes.

Outside, I let the wind raise
the tips of their feathers
before lifting them to brightness,
then stood on heavy legs
as they shrank to a point in memory.

The wonder was they came back,
even when there were more of them:
iridescent necks and bobbing heads
in the driveway, then on the clothesline,
where they wait for me still

to swing open the heavy doors
that have closed behind me
where I stand now
looking up for lost wonder
as if into the same sky.

Celebration

At first distracting
as an old typewriter,
the squirrel taps
across the tin roof
of my back porch,

then leaps to the dracaena
where our eyes meet
and I call, as I always do,
"Hello, friend, how are you?"

A clump of dry weeds in his mouth,
he's off again, a light drum roll
across the neighbor's carport,

and finally the rustle of leaves
as he disappears into the dense ivy
which climbs all the way to the top
of the fan palm separating the two homes.

It's been several days now
without the usual coastal fog,
smudges of pink clouds chalking
a still-blue, late September sky,
just before night—with its tempered applause
by a few faithful stars—falls,

leaving me uneasy but hopeful
that, if cautious, I can find
the first of five steps leading up to the door,
one more of those tiny surprises of existence.

Woodpiles Revisited:
When the Words Came

How could he know at ten
that it wasn't his father's
exacting orders he obeyed
each time he was told to reassemble
the pile of scrap lumber
against the greenhouse wall,
toiling in solitude, satisfying
a nameless urge not with words
but with shapes rejected
by someone else to his fresh purpose.

He liked how they occupied space
after surrendering to his hands,
an accommodation of solid objects
that had refused to yield unless they
were allowed to take the lead.
All because he looked again
at what he had seen—length and width,
thickness and angle—until
it told his hands what to do.

Later, when the words came
with their hard edges
they would take him back
to that space between
himself and what he perceived,
and he would wait there
until he felt them moving under his hands.

RL

A Place in the Sun

This morning when I saw our dog
curled up in a square of sunlight
on the living room floor, I thought
briefly of Montgomery Clift,

his gloomy quest in the film
that co-opted the phrase.
But quickly that image faded
and I skipped back to the time

before I had seen a desert
and dreamt during arithmetic
of a sand expanse stretching north
up the sunlit slope of my desk

until it fell off into the Grand Canyon,
reminded then that all I needed to do
was step out the creaky double door
of our one-room schoolhouse

to track down my own place in the sun
that moved with the seasons
up and down hills, through oak groves
and fields, or only a few steps

beyond our backyard chicken coop,
under a cluster of sumac, where
magically in the dead of winter
I could stretch out on a cushion of

green and reach for a handful
of snow. Or wait for an afternoon
in early spring to wander down
to the brook at the base of the slope →

to watch bright civilizations of
salamanders go about their lizardly business
in patches of watery brilliance
just beyond the shadow of the overhang

that lengthened as I lay there
until the sun was gone, and they with it.

Crossing the Line

Though the trail of breadcrumbs grows faint,
I still limp ahead toward some vague line
I say I won't cross when I get there.

Just now it's spring and under the mesquite
and creosote a sparrow leaves the feeder
to prance and puff before a ready mate.

And tomorrow I'll leave my winter home
in the Sonoran Desert, my family, the few friends
I hold dear like a last, short candle,

and the goldfinch, the portly quail,
cardinal, dove, and cottontail
that scurries in and out of the shadows at dawn and dusk,

hesitant as a child in a room full of strangers.
This has been my delight these last four months,
but I'm heading west, back to the Central Coast

where the sirens of the sea call
like my father's two-fingered whistle at dinnertime,
back to my modest roof in a town

whose Riviera prices I can ill-afford
and the trailer park where that unfortunate phrase,
that hyphenate of *trash*, first became a moniker.

I think about the line again,
of the indolence there among the tweakers
and alcoholics, so dulling

that seaslugs appear to race across tidemarks,
toadstools across the forest floor.
It's a thousand miles I used to drive non-stop; →

but I'm aging fast, those marathon days
more difficult, the line moving closer and closer,
this trip a two-nighter, the first in Kingman,

the second Mojave, two towns with the allure
of a landfill. I'll stop in the sizzling
afternoon heat, get a first floor room,

search out a daily paper, flip on the tube and AC,
kick back, pretending to enjoy myself,
then the next morning, my pockets nearly empty of mustard seed,

gas up, scrape the yellow bugs from my windshield,
hit the road again, over the Tehachapis,
coming to the drum of the surf, to my father's shrill whistle.

II

What the Flowers Need to Know

Distance

The squirrel on the porch in the brightness
of midmorning looks like any other.
But she keeps coming back, circling closer,
until I'm forced to notice coarse gray hairs,
an awkward thickness in the hips.
She waddles to the edge of the deck,
lies facing the distance,
hind legs splayed, like our pug.

As she returns I discover
fur on sides and back
delicately scalloped like feathers,
tail vaguely striped black.
Now, ten feet off, on heavy
haunches, she chews. Her jaws
and cheeks pulse with grace.
She holds one eye on me—
a shadow behind glass, retreating
to the absolute distance of words.

Mourning Doves

What god were they
to the Greeks

that still moans
in whitewash heat,

bearing old grief
through hedges

to darken our rooms
with childhood gone,

lost love, generations
spent on change

when nothing
changes, the hedge

still in flower,
the bird still lovely

wooing the moment,
what happy god?

Home

Often traveling thirty miles
from roost to feeding grounds,
they know which side
their toast is buttered on,
these crows that cruise
this desolate stretch of Highway 58
between Mojave and Barstow.

The same cannot be said
for the owl, apparently building a nest
somewhere in Golden Gate Park,
found this morning
at the foot of a utility pole,
a piece of metal conduit
still in her beak, her face an open flower,
while 80,000 homes go without
coffee and toast for breakfast.

I imagine her spotting that prize—
that glint of metal—the day before,
then waiting for the cover of darkness
to swoop in and snatch
what might have looked,
at that necessary moment in her life,
like rebar for brick and mortar.

Lacking Anything Swift

Today a whitewinged dove
collided with the dining room window,
left a spray of pale yellow
on the tinted pane.
He lay stunned a long while—
he must have been flying at full speed
when he confused the reflected scene
with his future. His crop
had burst; tiny black seeds
clung to breast feathers.
He was as handsome as any pigeon.

We wanted to forgive him
his most human mistake,
hose down the glass,
wipe his feathers clean,
see him off.
But his eyes were opaque
and after long minutes
he couldn't move.
On the telephone
we were advised
to use a shovel,
lacking anything swift.

When he veered off, flapping,
in the middle of our chores,
he hardly cleared the greasewood.
But he had recovered enough
to grow alert, command his pain;
we could hope for more.
If not, most people hereabout
have dogs, and after dark
coyotes roam the hollows in packs.

Messages

I guess if you imagine
my eyes the sun,
my girth the earth,
and the toilet bowl the moon,
there is a partial lunar eclipse
every time I stand at the john,
which of late, what with a prostate
the size of a Tuscan melon,
is damned often and always urgent.

In fact, just yesterday,
when a chunky lizard,
who'd been scooting along
the crown of my adobe wall,
suddenly stopped—
within my immediate purview,
mind you,
in what was perhaps
some courting ritual
with an unseen mate—
and began doing pushups,
I, with the unassailable logic
of an aging adult,
assumed it was a message
aimed directly at me. →

I went inside,
flipped on March Madness,
poured a 24-ounce tumbler of tangerine juice,
slapped a cinnamon swirl
as big as a Frisbee
on an enamelware plate and sank,
along with any resolve,
into the old corduroy chair,
my grumpy arches ready for a siesta
on the matching ottoman.
The problem was
I had trouble deleting
an earlier message
from the Inca dove I'd found
dead the day before
at the foot of the same wall,
lying on its back,
its little pink legs and feet,
stiff as new boots,
but still on, mind you,
and pointed up through the olive branches
directly toward the heavens.

Windows

1

My mother-in-law called
to report that for the first time
in years she heard something
in her right ear: voices
floating like an absolution
through her bedroom window.

So what if it was also
the last time. Some people
with their full senses
keep the windows shut all day.

2

My own mother suffered
from a one-way heart.
Everything kept pouring out,
but she couldn't find
where the opening was
to let anything back in.

3

When we lived in the country
we left our windows uncovered.
The hummingbirds didn't seem
to mind. Here we have drapes,
though they aren't needed,
with six-foot patio walls. →

When I wake I pull back
the curtains and look up
at the same piece of sky,
knowing it's been waiting for me
all night while I pondered
what Stephen Hawking had to say
about what is apt to pour in
when our expectations
are reduced to zero.

Morning Stretch

On my back in the living room,
legs bent, hands tugging at my thighs
trying to dissolve a knot in my hip,
happy to be distracted by
Chopin's *Fantaisie-Impromptu*,

I start paying attention to the notes,
their utter clarity, how like bells
they deliver in pristine isolation
the sounds he chose to release
from their galactic swirl into the
measured harmony of common breath

while I hold on,
fingers wrapped behind knees,
in a morninglit room
where clocks have no hands
in a world where rocks
beside trees turn to sand.

Euclid and Leaves

If he were heading south
toward the bay,
he'd look like the number seven
tacking into an on-shore breeze.

But he's walking north,
bent at the waist
as if following some scent,
his torso parallel to the pavement,
his eyes missing the only patch of blue
in a gray November sky.

My left eye tears, strains to focus
through failed surgery,
distance blurred like words on a coin
shimmering in the deep end of a pool.

Poor guy, I think as I pass,
trying to imagine life so stooped—
the angles of his longing,
the axis of his needs—
pitying for a second
what I don't think now needed pity.

I should have stopped, turned,
walked with him across the intersection,
telling him of a black bird I make out
just landed in the maple,
while he marvels at the yellow leaves
crackling beneath our feet—
as if we each
might comfort the other
with our secrets,
as if this were all
either of us ever asked for.

Explaining the Landscape to a Squirrel

The last two days I've found you sitting
near the shed in a corner of the fence,
head and shoulders propped above the cedar slats.
You pose, your back to the house, with all
the smugness of a lifeguard, with the dignity
of the god who controls the local harvest.

How long have you known about the view?
Are you too dreaming in the foothills,
wondering if any of it's real?
If you could use our telescope as we do
when we lower our sight, you'd see
signboards on the freeway, the K-Mart emblem
and Exxon, a sanitary landfill, the honest
green of flowing sewage; behind you,
in layers, flattened hills, steep drives,
trim homes an acre apart, and residents
who move through lavender like silhouettes.

Sometimes before a storm the mountains
directly behind your head show their depth.
Halfway into the hills a poet
keeps her world alive with stories of Coyote,
of distant people made real by the sun.
The crags beyond hold places to crawl into,
where all that we've forgotten unfolds
in the dark, like notes from a flute.

Dead Grass

He sees the grasshopper before he thinks of himself.
It is thick and clumsy, as if grown for two lifetimes
and is missing something mental or carries
something extra that its brain can't figure out.
Unlike the delirious insects of his youth, it lacks
the will to flash its underside sailing off,
but rolls to avoid the hoe, stutters toward weeds
wilting in the gravel, nudges under them,

allows him time to think of the keyboard,
imagine his fingers working around the points of pain
left by cactus needles inside his gloves,
clutching the metaphor that satisfies
because it is complete, though never understood,
and will disappoint, describing him, a memory
of himself clenching a hoe, tossing dead grass
into the alley to be shaped by the wind.

Deliverance

The temperature is twelve degrees Fahrenheit,
the dirt road covered in ice and new snow,
wind-driven, and slashing across a meadow,
then through a break in a long stand of ponderosa.

On this Christmas Eve, a woman leans
against the elements and the night,
pushing her bike with its tote
through the last two miles of backcountry
toward the outskirts of Pinetop,
a mountain village on the Mogollon Rim.

Though heading in the opposite direction,
I stop, offer her a lift back to town,
which she politely refuses, taking instead
a ten dollar bill I had stuffed in the console of my truck.
I nod as I pull away, imagining her for a moment
warmed by the glow of my taillights.

After all, she wore only a shirt and jeans,
her coat wrapped around a small dog
that sat obediently in a baby seat,
his eyes squinting in the unforgiving air,
his tongue brighter than probability,
trusting her to deliver them both
from this onslaught of winter.

I think of the holiday carol and the lyricist
who wrote, "The weather outside is frightful,"
the operative word "outside," for inside
is a crackling juniper fire,
a rocker pulled close to the hearth,
ragg wool socks and elkskin slippers…
perhaps smoke from a sweet briar pipe
encircling the dim room of a cabin. →

What would it take, I ask myself,
to learn to love the austerity
of this woman and her dog,
alone and homeless as they are,
yet not lonely, each step careful, purposeful,
doubt, for them, too thin a fuel to run on.

Reflections at Laguna Beach

These gulls that strut pink legs
to make children giddy between tides
don't know indifference, nor do waves
ever tire of dissolving into spray
or carving hollows into bluffs,
reviving the Earth in ventricular chambers
just below the point, where a teenage girl
poses for her father, blonde and erect
between a crumbling shoreline and concrete stairs.

Migrant pigeons pick at battered shells,
eccentric, as bright as the first
to fidget through traffic in Providence
or the one that teetered for a photo
in San Marco Square, one leg snagged
in someone's hair, a foil to glinting sunset.

They go barely noticed, soft in their feathers,
their shine reflected in sheets of sand, retrievable,
but only by something preceding memory
that resists words, penetrates
the haze of our conceptions,

suspends a grayfaced man above the point
as he leans back toward the bank's contorted growth,
steadies himself, and rotates his camera
to preserve something, the ocean's falling pulse,
in the fragile instant of a smile.

Beach Scene at Tropea, with Moon

A tattooed Italian couple
flirt on the pebbled shore
where Odysseus and his brooding men
might have caught their breath
under wind-scarred cliffs
that now buttress the ancient town.

Dressed for the street, a tiny Asian woman
hawks beach towels in English,
her thin voice cracking the salt air.

A youngish father wearing a Yankees cap
sits up, roused from noon languor
by his daughter's shrieks of wonder
fronting waves for the first time.

Beyond, barely noticed, a thin-haired man,
knees bent in surf, snaps
pictures of his middle-aged wife.

Maybe he's trying to frame
the way he wants to remember her.
Maybe he's equally in love with the ocean.
Whatever the reason, she goes along with it.

Moments ago she was an ordinary tourist
dressed a little fancy for the beach.
Now she steps lightly in the foam, laughs
in his direction, throws her head back
each time she lifts her pleated skirt

to take another step out
toward Stromboli's hazy shoulder
lifted on the horizon, then stops
just where the water shows—
will always show—dark
against her white thighs,
like night surrounding the moon.

Tsunami

What did that solitary figure see
as he stood in the surf,

the first great wave breaking
then surging around him?

Did he imagine a wife
sitting on the edge of a bed

in a hotel room not forty yards
over his left shoulder?

Was she putting sunscreen
on her thighs and midriff

before joining him
at water's edge?

Or did he see a daughter
away at school in Ann Arbor,

chilled between classes
by the raw cold in another hemisphere?

I wonder, did he wish to flee,
to take some magical step

back in time? Or picture
in that last moment

his lungs rising like pheasant
into a perfect blue sky?

Maybe the earth slowed,
its moon wheeling

farther and farther away
in the screaming eddies,

in the grind of the rip tides.
I would like to think

he saw nothing—
his mind unable to fathom

the enormity of that wall of water,
that tumult,

that hugeness
closing him out—

his life simply awash
in the pale colors before sleep.

Alaska

This is no place even for the young, they say,
where the body shudders
and the wind blows so hard
you never breathe the same air twice.

That may be so, but the old still come,
if only to try it on their tongues, confirm
that it's always the same air,
even when their arches cramp

and sagging back muscles
cling to the nearest bone—
while the days grow short
and they keep talking like old sailors

addressing everyone: waves of
youthful faces rolling over rapids,
those left behind to age at home
or hunched in alleys,

and those like themselves
who choose to keep drifting,
learning to live with words
before losing them in the dying wind.

The Scream

It cannot come from a fresh face
that has not yet met sorrow,
a squeal sliding from the foliage of childhood
like a caterpillar soon to metamorphose
and scribble across a blue page of sky.

But since the stroke,
it is the only sound she can make—
and it could shatter crystal.
It rises like wasps
from some deep abscess
at the core of her mortality
and when it finds her tongue
at the nursing home, its sting
splinters the stale air around her.

If her wrists weren't tethered
to the arms of a wheelchair,
she would pull out her hair,
something that fierce still in her eyes,
what the fires have left of the temple.
It is a sound older than words,
an acknowledgment of the first gulp of air
and the last.

RL

That Day

Something is approaching in silence—
a heatless object floating in space,
a condor toward the smell of death.

We cringe in place, ears stunned
by what they don't hear, hold our breath,
as if any gesture could intercept the trajectory

of hate. The last few inches of infinity
collapse and the present leaps to our screens
in horrific silence and flashes away

to converge, in the guise of pain, with galaxies.

* * *

Something has been presented and taken away
before there is time to extract ourselves
from our own clumsiness. Its shadow

pins us down. And once again
we succumb to abstractions, as if
they could be turned face up and counted

or weighed thousands of tons
and could crash into themselves
in silence, in unspeakable silence.

Confluence

Two friends, each on the other's birthday,
call to offer good wishes, to ask
what insights have been gleaned from the year just past.

Once, Connie answered, "I've learned to love what is.
But, ohsweetjesus, they've found colon cancer."
Another time, Sarah said, "Nobody else
is going to do it, and, by the way,
I can't open a can of tomato soup."

And since no one asked me last June,
I'll dialogue with myself, as I often do,
try to get things in order,
gather my thoughts for the next report.

I learned, dear self, that the world is broken,
that cyberspace is another name for sandstorm,
the windshield of human discourse pocked,
disfigured beyond recognition,
that cell phones hate mountains, bridges, and valleys,
and that I would have preferred smoke signals.

I've learned that the engines and menus of commerce
don't really make the world go choo choo,
that they're less secure than a styrofoam cup
snagged in tumbleweed at the side of the road,
that fiber optics foreshadow shallow breath, toxic rivers
and acid rain rushing
through the ruins of our monuments.

I've learned that for many in power
compassion is a chip of petrified wood
looted from the mesas of the past,
that America speaks again with a forked tongue,
and that god lives in Des Moines. →

I've learned that vindictiveness
has an abacus for a brain
and—behind a sweet veneer,
just to the left of the breastbone—
a lump of coal as big as your fist for a heart.

I've learned that my daughter loves a woman
and know that the quail and dove,
the goldfinch, cardinal, and woodpecker
have been well-fed this cold winter.

And a few months from now,
down the road apiece, on the equinox,
I'll run head-on into seventy-six
at the confluence of desire and despair,
loathing and joy, on the other side
of that roiling white water
the slot machines of uncertainty
chortling day and night.

On that special day, I'll call my pod—
that diaspora of love and flesh and ash,
some scattered before their time,
that tiny clutch more tenacious than ivy—
I'll call on a land line far from the nearest box store
and say, "Ah ha. Our days are numbered. We're dying.
I love you. Today is the first day of summer."

RL

Time

We make it up every day,
counting minutes and hours
like shifting furniture.

It gives us a way to talk:

I put my shoes on
before I walk the dog.
We can't eat bacon
till they shoot a hog.

and the only reason to fear:

We know where we've been
though not where we'll be
when disaster hits our town
or a hijacked plane goes down
the day we depart for Spain.

It's always now or then
that holds us here or there.
That's why we try to shun our pain,
usurp the blind unfolding, and why
(help me with this, nardo)

some mothers drown their babies
and fathers torch their little girls
to counter their despair.

Trust

It was last night
as I nursed a second failed surgery—
the periphery of my vision
blanched with whiteout,
circumscribed within
starbursts from the dimmest light—
that I had to look away
from the evening news,
story after story
of the chilling failures of our species:

The infant daughter
of a drunk and desperate mother
immolated in a microwave;
that ceaseless violence in the Middle East,
that cauldron we continually stoke:
bombs and beheadings,
blood and bone
staining the dust, the asphalt
at every treacherous turn.

And those shameful vignettes
of the lucky ones, the legless,
the armless, the faceless, the insane,
those who do not sleep
because they know what they'll dream,
come home, dumped in rooms
infested with rats and roaches,
the peeling paint on the walls
a metaphor for the dead skin
of deceit and betrayal.

This morning, a harsh winter rain
soaks an unwrapped newspaper
thrown heedlessly
into the deepest rut of my driveway.
I lift it, the weight astonishing,
and wonder how we survive,
buried alive as we often are
when the heart of the world is broken.

We go back—don't we?—
over and over again
to what we have learned to trust,
in our pockets totems of the journey:
a bear claw, a guitar pick, a cowrie,
some message,
an epiphany long ago
on a deserted beach in Mexico.

We scatter seed
for the quail and dove,
funnel thistle for the finches,
cage a slab of suet
for the woodpecker and cactus wren,
then, leaning on an adobe wall,
still as a Seri carving,
wait—like kids
holding their breath for Santa—
for the red splash of a cardinal
among the thin branches of creosote and olive. →

Later, we will sweep feathers and down
from the patio floor—
a cat, perhaps, or Cooper's hawk
with their hunger, their own wild selves?—
and realize this is our place…
here near the dark center of the maze,
the trembling core of consent,
here where we measure years
with the return of brooding doves,
with novenas for a dead brother and son,
where we stand, somehow chastened,
our eyes opening wider,
and try to save what little
we hope can be saved.

What the Flowers Need to Know

Who was the one who lay on his side last night,
hair drying to straw, ear pressed to pillow, thin-skinned
skull cupped in his own hand? Poor Yorick-to-be,

whispered awake at dawn by flowers outside the window
with the news: There's still time to watch from this side
the Earth unfolding and like God love it enough to say

nothing as it is plundered by greed, crushed under
rubble, soaked with the blood of innocence—because
too many believe in something other than each other.

But the blooms on the arching shoot need to be told they
are the reason you won't let go—and you as well, entranced
by this world, but not enough to embrace the unlovable.

You could tell them that's just the way it is when you
draw life from two worlds and the one you desire more
is the one you can step outside and breathe in.

Ghosts

Sometimes he stands at the edge of their bed,
his left hand reaching for hers,
but when she sits up, breaching the darkness,
and calls his name,
he glides back as if on tracks
toward the closet door,
disappearing as quickly as a smoke ring.

Do some linger, as the whisperers believe,
after they have leapt from the body,
turning their backs to the insistent light
that will guide their drift to another world,
staying behind a little longer
to tend to the living,
who often must learn to stand,
to walk, to eat, to sleep,
even to breathe again?

Or do we in our loss
try to plumb coincidence
with the precision of a Euclidean proof,
any tortured logic to make the invisible visible?
A crow circles the backyard memorial
for a friend's father
and she knows, therefore, he has not yet gone,
that he will follow her home,
each molted feather forever a sigh;
or, perhaps, you find in that ribbon
of tumbled shell and kelp
marking the night's high tide
a cowrie, a message left at your feet by your son,
not a hundred yards, mind you,
from where a year before
you scattered his ashes in the Sea of Cortez.

Just now, we long for certitudes,
a sign, a symbol, some presence
that has been with them
or come from them—
Oh, how we want to believe
that we might reach beyond the ruin,
through the numbed silence of their absence
to that place where parallel lines do intersect,
stretching in our thinnest armor
toward the sanctuary of horizon
as if for a lottery ticket, a perfect apple.

III

Afloat Between Margins:
The Soul's Circus

Old love,

it's so familiar: lying on our backs,
elbows dug into the cold sand
of a desert wash, a mesquite fire crackling

at our feet, and a Tibetan bowl, its song
rising into the galaxy, the Milky Way so thick
I could have scraped it from the sky,

rubbed it across your shoulders like lotion,
then, with the precision of a watchmaker,
placed a clandestine kiss on the nape of your neck.

We were young, all cylinders on go,
the emergency brake off as we gained speed,
barreling down the steep hills of foolishness and lust.

But seeing you last night across the table—
a friend distanced by a thousand miles
and how many years, close to twenty?—

you, dear lady, still beautiful, smiling
when a little girl weaved in and out among the diners,
flapping her arms as she sang,

"See, I'm flying like a bird";
you, the coy mistress, aglow like a pumpkin,
a carriage I'd love to reserve again for the night,

the two of us toasting life and poetry and the past,
our jaws clenched so tightly around the word future
that we might have broken glass—

the little girl and her magic,
the two of us so much older and wiser
certain that at midnight the spell always ends.

RL

After the Workshop

When you read your poems
aloud, said the sage poet,
they sound better
than they actually are.

That night he dreamed of margins,
a narrow stage
preserving the exact place
where Hamlet left off
and Olivier began, recognized
the expansive genius of Chopin
in the tapering fingers
of Horowitz, watched as a spotlight
trained on Puccini
wearing the face of Leontyne Price.

Numb with another gray morning,
he saw words that had
glowed on his tongue
shrink to notes on paper
and thought back forty years, wondering,
when he secretly swooned
over Elizabeth Barrett Browning,
if it was really the ancient Miss Jenkins,
with her pink scalp and prominent incisors,
who, having spent decades
practicing modulation
through her six-foot frame,
embodied his romantic ideal.

In the new dream
there is moonlight
but no moon, a lover
revived in her sickbed
by the sound of her own voice,
looking past her beloved
to gaze on words
roaming outside the moment
toward a distant intimacy, a fervor
in the breath of voices
she will never hear.

Fortune Cookie

Times are tough when you turn
to a fortune cookie for survival tips.
Take my knees, for example,
so cranky, badgered with arthritis,
I've had to puddle my pants on the floor,
try to step into each leg with the grace
of someone playing hopscotch in a potato sack.
I thought I'd win a kewpie doll
when I finally cinched them to my waist.

And if it's not that -*itis*
it's another, my eyes at times
so dry and brittle they're kaleidoscopic,
pieces of glass tumbling,
chattering into bright geometries
each time I turn my head.

There's less detail now,
just the contour of things;
the russet pillow
on the back of my easy chair
looks at ten paces
like a horseshoe with edema;
and the old stump of an Aleppo pine
in the front yard might be a butte
rising in the distance outside Shiprock.

Things break along the way—
bones and china bowls,
marriages and meerschaums,
hearts, necks, of course lives,
now your body *en masse*.
And nothing will make you whole again,
not designer drugs, carpenter's glue,
vitamins, duct tape, braces, prayer.

All you can do is cherish each crack,
revere every rip and shard,
mount them in the album of your days
and turn the page—with help if need be.

Put up with small annoyances,
the fortune cookie read,
to gain great results.

Well, I can't go quite that far
but I remember Chumley,
a friend's old bull-mastiff,
who, the day after cancer took
his right front leg to the shoulder,
wandered into my yard
then lifted a hind leg at his favorite juniper
as if the laws of physics had been repealed.

Intimations

The day did come when something fell away.
I can't say exactly what day it was
because when that happens it's like
moving past any bright noon
when your skin goes dry with the grass,
unnoticed. A sparrow in that moment
becomes a sparrow on the lawn.
Salamanders in the brook nearby
lose their spots on the speckled floor,
shadows of trout stiffen.
Whales sink into their bulk, mere whales.
Horseshoe crabs vanish one last time
in a puff of sand. And seagulls whirl away
through sullen corners of light, their calls
retreating with troops of pigeons,
familiars of fallen grace.

But who's to say anything,
above or below, has been diminished
when ordinary dawns brighten
with anticipation, when what has faded
returns with the force of exotic memory—
as much to torment as to please me,
wandering deserts and swamps
in the last days of my imagination,
marching wordless and throbbing through jungles,
a photographer without a camera,
expecting something in the sky
to flash and hold, flash and
hold me where I am.

Truancy

I didn't want to get out of bed
so, like a kid playing hooky,
I lay there reading a Jack London novel
secretly encrypted in the grains and knots
of a pine wall across the room.

A flock of snow geese headed south
and the eye of a brown trout was unmistakable
as the fish rose for a fly at dusk
from a wild river running through a gorge
whose ragged tablets of sedimentary history covered eons.

Yesterday, I told Susan I'd yanked a poem
from the first chapter of a new manuscript
and she thought I said, "I yanked out my chest tube,"
which isn't that far-fetched,
my wheeze vibrating lately like a didgeridoo.

Nancy would be drinking latte alone
if I didn't get my carcass in gear
but I looked for any excuse
to stay under the covers a bit longer,
hold back another day like the tide
threatening a sand castle I'd labored over.

So I began a new game, more demanding, cerebral:
What am I going to do, I asked myself, when…?
When the cortisone wears off?
When I can't open a can of chicken soup
or make my bed? When I can't drive to Lotus Garden
for some righteous moo shu or almond duck?
What am I going to do when a guest finds
my one-and-only Hustler buried
under a stack of AARP bulletins? →

My yin and yang went through a messy divorce in the '90's,
one heading to Amsterdam, the other Death Valley.
And my libido, my libido hitched a ride
out of town autumns ago on a winged chariot
disguised as a three-wheeled electric scooter named Go-Go.
I'm so out of touch, I think *svelte*
is a processed cheese food or Norwegian sardine.

I try to slow time down, stop it in its tracks,
but it keeps on clicking as it crosses my sights
like shooting-gallery ducks—*plink,*
another trash pickup; *plink, plink,*
another utility bill; *plink, plink, plink,*
another rainy season, another drought,
another Christmas, another auld lang syne.
It's relentless, and I don't know what I'll do.

Surely the conveyer belt will shred at any moment,
but because I'd indulged myself—
lost in the wilderness of irony for forty minutes,
lying there spent from the hunt—
I knew time's truant officer would nab me
if my feet didn't touch the floor,
step through the broken glass
of sunlight just below my bed,
if my Pilot pen didn't begin to scribble
madly across this yellow notepad.

RL

Late Bloomer, Too Late

He's past feeling like an unexpected rose.
Too late to win esteem like Abraham,
Cervantes, or Grandma Moses.
He can't help feeling he's under
a short sentence, a drowning man
begging for someone to take back everything,
beginning with the wrong plunge,
the current spinning the car
that holds him under, the tree
he'd swerved to miss, the child
who distracted him, the license
that permitted more than a drive
through woods, the town
where he lived in a bungalow
at the end of a solemn street, and words
that make every thing what it is,
knowing now the only need he ever had
was to start over with none of it
so he could have it all.

Pepper

Call me first, I said
to my post-op ride,
make sure I survived the surgery.
Then I chuckled,
and then he chuckled,
good, hearty belly-laughs
before he added,
Yeah, cousin, don't you dare
stand me up.

But beneath the joke,
the uneasy deceit,
there on a rainy evening in late October,
a truth was being told,
passed back and forth between us
like a baseball
in a warm-up drill of pepper.

Pushing seventy-five
more and more
the nervous spectator,
sometimes I imagine I've missed
a million flies in a row.

One more look, I say,
as if mysteriously out of place,
as if there can't be
an excuse for everything,
one more chance
to pound my glove
and fill the night with wonder.

RL

Interlude, After Surgery

I thought I was waiting
for it all to come back
in vibrant August.

But the call of a jay
on a pale afternoon, an invisible jay
scolding someone

or some thing
in another direction
told me I was the one

who had to come back
where sights and sounds waited
in a sudden lovely world.

MRI

Maybe the headaches will explain the blank spaces
where words seem to have dropped out
or were left behind while the poems groped on
through cloudbanks, never to return to that place,
aptly named a terminal, where their parts waited
like errant luggage, and even if they could,
never to know what they were looking for,
what pieces were missing, and what all that
would add up to once it came together.

As if it weren't hard enough to answer that question
when one of them comes out whole, held intact
by some membrane that grows out of itself,
completely cut off from the brain's tissue,
which never stops scanning for its own voice
to preserve what it thinks is something else.
Even now, when it hears only incessant knocking.

Aubade

In the dream, my nephew has a raging toothache
but no money, no insurance,
so I do the best I can in this anxious age,
rummaging through the medicine cabinet
for oil of clove.

And my daughter, somewhere amidst
the atrophied ventricles of my brain,
sobs softly to her mother,
just home from abroad,
that she can't see retirement

even with a telescope,
that Social Security and Medicare,
already flimsy as a child's balsa glider,
will explode and burn as they enter
the profitably toxic atmosphere

of this fourteenth year of a new millennium.
In the dream the dogs haven't been fed
and I can't remember
if I stashed their food
in my safe deposit box or a low-interest C.D.

Suddenly a siren wails in the distance
and I whisk cobwebs from my face and shoulder,
a trespasser in the basement
of, might I hope, someone else's nightmare
where sorrow mottles the walls like mold.

But even in sleep, my son is snagged in time,
almost forty years later yet forever thirteen,
still on his bicycle in the middle
of that nasty intersection in San Jose,
simply distracted for a moment →

by the complexities of a first kiss.
Then, finally, the last grainy frame of this dream
having flicked by—always
his reckless, understated smile the trailer—
and despite some hopeless,
human message in the blood,
I throw back the covers
to a splendid concoction of dawn,
telling myself, as if an aside,
This is the chance of a lifetime.

RL

Afloat Between Margins

Floaters: Specks that appear to float before the eyes,
caused by defects or impurities in the vitreous humor.
Webster's New World Dictionary

The first one wobbled into daylight,
hooked up with a flimsy cloud,
then drifted like an abandoned skiff
toward a dim shore, where it shrank
to paramecium size, reversed direction,
corkscrewed under a microscope,

and disappeared when I rubbed my eyes
to restore the universe, a familiar scale
for my thoughts, musing all the while
on the ancient Romans, how feeling
detached from the orderly world
they must have staved off terror,

domesticating fear with two humble words,
muscae volitantes, flies that fly
in the marketplace or at the casement,
like the one now making a slow loop
across a luminous window shade,
getting hung up on a spider's line

and swinging there a while
before metamorphosing to a jellyfish
that sails a straight line westward
toward a cave no doubt, offscreen,
which releases bats one at a time
until sunset. →

In the fading light,
imagination rubbed out by the daylong
procession of acrobatic shapes, I look out
on a scene with its own familiar shading,
where I regard myself once more
shadowed among creatures,

not as one blot among many
drifting toward trees and annihilation.
Gradually my eyes widen to greet darkness
as it absorbs the last apparition
before I sleep, afloat between the margins
of every beginning and every end.

Slash

I'm sitting on the closed lid
of my oak toilet seat, which is
fairly new, the old one broken a few years ago
when I fell, my blood glucose punching 1400.

Anyway, I'm sitting here, legs crossed,
a clever little paddle in my hand,
sanding away at the cracked heels of my feet,
the rutted gator-hide of my elbows,

with the careful intent of a cabinet-maker.
And it's hard at this moment
not to think of my own mortality,
the slash and sawdust of life

right here in front of me or not—
an amputated middle toe,
a bonsai'd, jointless grand toe,
each day rushing at me faster and faster,

a runaway 18 wheeler on an 8% downgrade,
its driver cranked on methamphetamine.
This is tough stuff, I tell myself,
sanding away, my 75-year-old bony ass

and arthritic, discless spine whining
across the sciatic notch
in an unpleasant, nervous falsetto.
I wonder if everyone in the world

has lost a brother or sister,
a son or daughter. Do we all
schlep along with that kind of missing baggage?
And I wonder also if there are any words →

I might conjure up, then rehearse—
astonishment of late
ever so hard to come by—
that will adequately explain to my daughter

why I do not want her
to pluck like overnight, forest toadstools
the wild, white, brazen hairs
sprouting now from my eyebrows.

RL

Heard from a Compassionate
CT Scanner in an Unsettled Time

Breathe in...Hold your breath.
Stop thinking, dream. Know
without a job you are the same person.
Your passions live in your breath.
B r e a t h e.

Hold your breath.
Forget that your mortgage is
underwater. Swim
with affectionate angelfish.
B r e a t h e.

Hold your breath.
Ignore what Wall Street took away.
Pretend you won the lottery
or inherited a cabaret.
B r e a t h e.

Hold your breath.
Banish the thought of going
bankrupt. Be a child again
skipping jail in Monopoly.
B r e a t h e.

Hold your breath.
Forget the rubble in Afghanistan.
Make plans to raise the roof
with your Amish neighbors.
B r e a t h e.

Hold your breath.
Stop counting starving children
in Sudan. Let your spirit
join theirs and together dream.
B r e a t h e. →

Hold your breath.
Avoid the stalled traffic on the freeway.
Your life awaits you,
an open road. Take it now.
B r e a t h e.

RL

The Soul's Circus

> "Only God knows our real names."
> – James Hillman, quoted by Thomas More

A task I've been putting off
has stepped on my spirit
as if to tell me who I am,
overruling the universe,

so I look out on this gusty morning
for some way to shake off the night,
watch a towering ponderosa
halfway down the slope

wave its creaky limbs
while tiny birdshapes pulse black
against the orange
of shimmering cliffs.

But all that goes on
without me. My spirit,
shrunk to a world too small
for stars, has lost its way.

I feel like an adult
at a circus, caught
in the depths of compulsion
as chipmunks flip

like jesters in the piñon
growing through our deck,
one of them riding a birdfeeder
that rotates liquid pink →

on my face. Objects hanging
from rafters join in:
Pewter dolphins swim in circles,
copper monkeys swing

by their tails, elephants spin
amid the swirl of gongs and chimes.
The wind rules the dance.
And only the wind

knows the path
that wanders through time
before me—the holy path
that leads to who I am.

Prostates and Papayas

If anyone had told me ten years ago
I'd be wearing a Poise liner
in the crotch of my bikini briefs,
I'd have said in my best South Philly accent,
"Forget about it; that's a line I'll never cross."

But here I am at seventy-five,
my list of ailments growing longer
than the bar tab I racked up once
many New Year's Eves ago in North Beach:
Let's see, chronic kidney disease, stage 3;
lungs brittle as charred newsprint
with a stellate lesion on the rocks;
not to mention the stenosis
cracking like a buggy whip
across my cervical and lumbar spine;
finally, those pesky age-related bruises,
the color of merlot,
that mysteriously track my forearms
sometime during a restless night;
and, oh yes, as I hinted in the title,
a prostate the size of a papaya.

Still, I pry myself out of bed each morning
with a claw hammer of opiates,
unable to suppress a smile,
when I remember the cottontails
at dusk the night before—
so wary and shy and no bigger than a mitten—
coaxed from the shadows of creosote and Texas Ranger
by carrots in my sister's outstretched hand. →

And I know that, when the meds kick in,
I'll scatter seed for the quail and dove,
then stand like a rickety scarecrow,
flapping my arms to shoo off
the insistent Cooper's hawk
swooping in daily for breakfast
on the thermals of his own hunger.

Later, I will ooh and ahh as a full moon
rises like a biggah pizzah pie
above the Rincon Mountains,
that orb of lesser light
we entrust to rule what will be
a cold, end-of-February night.

The closer I get to dying, it seems,
the more I think about being here now,
this moment the gift,
everything else up for grabs—
a man with a wishbone clutched in his hand,
a man trusting that all he has to do
is make it through the next door he comes to,
a man, in his eighth decade,
able to look at his blood bruises again
and imagine a child's victory garden
ripe and dotted with eggplants.

One-legged Gull

He holds his own here
at the end of the wharf,
scavenging with the others
for scraps of old bait and bread.

And beneath the shrill din from this corps
of what must be a hundred screeching gulls,
I curse the nets, the discarded line
that probably took his leg.

I look down at my sandaled feet,
the middle toe on the right
lost to melanoma decades ago,
still hidden away in blue socks
from what I imagine to be
the uneasy stares of strangers.

But he'll have none of my anger, my shame
as he opens his wings and hops
to the top rail I lean on,
balancing there for a moment,
some ancient, abraded gargoyle,
some deity, perhaps, from the foundation of the world.

Then, suddenly, he lifts, wheels, and drops,
his flight deliberate, powerful
skimming along the surface of the bay
toward a patch of roiling water in the distance
where he alights
and, though paddling in circles,
feasts from a shoal of sardines. →

I turn in the morning mist,
shrug up my collar,
steady myself with a cane,
and head back in my own halting gait,
past Stagnaro's Fish Market, then Malio's Candies—
pain an ice pick stabbing deeper with every step—
past Castigliano's Grotto and Lillian's Gifts
toward my truck and Gilda's,
where I order the Lumberjack's Special,
flirt in spotty Italian with a cute Sicilian waitress,
sit awhile, able to forgive almost anything now
amidst the deep, throaty barks of sea lions,
the graceful, postcard glide of the pelican
and marvel that somehow—
broken and imperfect as we are, the gull and I—
the day has lavished us both with this.

RL

One More Poem About
What I Want to Say

Often of late I've Seen Li Po,
beloved writing companion
of the last twelve years,
standing in front of the doggie door
staring at nothing, as if
he'd forgotten what it was
he was about to do—
the way I too blank out
by the pantry or refrigerator.

What I don't forget is that it's age,
it's time, it's almost time
for one of us, or both.

And so I labor, tongue-tied, at my desk,
as if there's something words can do
while there *is* still time, knowing
there's nothing new about affliction.

I think of Sisyphus and Job,
dungeons, smoldering ghettos,
and vaster ghettos of the heart.
And you, still at it—even with Acorn gone,
tumbling with the others
in translucent waves of memory—
because the light comes back.

Because outside the window
each sunrise unravels history
and we turn undetected
like the leaves of vines,
learn how, when we look at things,
to see right through them to the Light.

Simplicity

I'm standing in the middle of the living room,
stopped mulishly in my tracks
with no idea of destination or purpose.
I remember where I was born,
my social security number,
the day's body count in Iraq,
and a few of my favorite cities—
Bergen, San Francisco, and one
that I think begins with a "G"—
but my sister's new mountain address,
the name of the waitress
I flirt with regularly at Gilda's
or any recollection
of whether I flossed my long teeth
a minute ago or not
teeter then lurch
in the dark vaults of my memory
like monarch butterflies
in a stand of eucalyptus.

Simplicity is necessary, I realize,
in order to go on even for a while.
So desperate am I
that I beg my dear and generous family/friends
not to put one more thing in my life
that can't be eaten in fifteen minutes or less.

I stand there
as if stunned by cold,
trying to make a deal
with a universe that was not—
contrary to the latest government report—
made with us in mind.

I stand there
and recall last weekend,
my six-month-old great granddaughter,
her shoes kicked off,
her pudgy fingers wrapped in rings
around her pudgy toes,
sitting in her car seat,
a baby Buddha cooing
from some fresh and secret mood,
while we ate chicken mole
at a beach-front café,
and though the years lean
crumpled in the corners of my day
like old umbrellas,
I know there is still room for this.

RL

The Heart's Song

Your heart doesn't know how old you are.
    −Heard on a television interview

Mine too keeps telling me I'm still
who I was, conspiring with memory
against time and winning the battle,
except when the mind steps back,
takes stock with narrowed eyes,
then moves through all its senses
to assess the sad situation: ears that
have lost touch with life's high notes,
nose dragging what's left of scent
through its own thicket, a tongue
that starts vacations at mealtime,
fingers gone numb except where nails
hang, and a departed prostate that has
vacated more than itself. Without doubt,
the mind gets the picture.

But this heart, stent-fed, held on
by sutures in four places, has its own sensor
that knows how to bypass insignificance
in the service of friendship, passion,
commiseration, learning to sing
in a universe that renews itself
while it is dying.

Tethered

Of course, it was impossible then
to know life would be unkind to him,
not in that chilled air
rich with the fragrance of cedar smoke
curling from a morning fire before which
his grandfather, moments earlier,
had warmed his jeans and shirt.

At three, he had come to realize
that a trike could get him only so far
and he tired of circling the first floor,
some tiny engine in his throat growling fiercely—
from the kitchen through the dining room
to the living room then back
after a u-turn in the foyer,
a rear hubcap invariably nipping
a sliver of mahogany from the front legs
of his mother's Victorian sofa.
He was tethered and going nowhere of consequence.

By the next summer, though,
long before he'd heard the words
torque and *vector*—
there was the whistling top he loved,
the gyroscope he spun endlessly on rainy days—
he began to dimly understand
the physics of it all,
that balance was a war between motion and gravity. →

So there he was, the rising sun at his back
as he straddled the two-wheeler—
a J.C. Higgins with balloon tires—
facing west toward the Delaware Bay,
his left foot planted in asphalt,
his right patting down the air for the pedal
which had to be set like clock hands
at precisely ten to ten.
He could feel his grandfather's breath
at his ear, his arthritic hand gripping the seat
as he trotted bent beside him now,
sand and gravel spitting from the tread,
a swarm of words encircling him like mosquitoes:
Don't let go pedal faster pedal faster don't let go.

And then, as he wobbled toward the horizon
under a canopy of hickory and oak,
red cedar and sassafras,
his own shadow coaxing him on,
the air suddenly became his friend
and he began to believe in himself
in a vast new way.

How could he have known
in that moment of delicious uncoupling,
that moment of sweet forever
which is the privilege of youth,
that the dead would never be
more than a breath or two
below his consciousness,
that every choice would be a sacrifice,
that his last tottering ride would be
a three-wheeled electric scooter
on a road which over his lifetime
would simply stretch then shrink,
inch by inch as it does now,
and go on without him?

About the Authors

RL

Robert Longoni grew up in New England and moved to Tucson as a teenager. He began his career at the University of Arizona, where he taught in the English Department for eleven years, including a stint as Director of the University's Poetry Center. In 1970 he joined the founding faculty of Pima Community College, where he helped set up the creative writing program and taught poetry writing along with other writing courses for more than twenty years. After his retirement in 1993, Bob and his wife, Vivian, spent parts of several years in the Zuni Mountains of New Mexico before returning permanently to Arizona, where they now live in Gilbert, a suburb of Phoenix. The landscapes of the various places where he lived provide the backdrop to many of his poems.

BCT

Trampled by pain each day, Bernardo Cristiani Taiz still enjoys a veal Milanese with linguine on the Santa Cruz Wharf and delights at the sea otters lounging with their catch in the hammock the swells of the bay provide. He avoids crowds and marvels at the geometry of spider webs. With Bob, he taught for thirty-plus years at the University of Arizona and Pima College, where he advised *Mazagine*, the college's literary/arts journal for which he was named Distinguished Adviser of the Year, 1977, by the National Council of College Publications Advisers. He was also the founding editor of Moon Pony Press in 1976, relinquishing those responsibilities a decade ago to younger, more energetic colleagues. He retired from academia in 1994 and is the author of three previous books: *What's a Mariachi Band Without a Trumpet? a Fun Writing Book*, along with two books of poems: *Something Soft to Land On* and *Digging with My Hands*.

Other Books by Moon Pony Press

None of This Will Kill Me, Jefferson Carter, 1987
History of Desire, Tony Hoagland, 1990
Woodpiles, Robert Longoni, 1997
How the World Is Given to Us, Barrie Ryan, 1998
The Swiftness of Crows, Nancy Wall, 1999
Creek Ceremony, Barrie Ryan, 2005
The Certainty of Looking Elsewhere, Mike Cassetta, 2009

Moon Pony Press
c/o Meg Files
PO Box 85394
Tucson AZ 85754

CPSIA information can be obtained
at www.ICGtesting.com
Printed in the USA
FSOW02n0317160715
8842FS